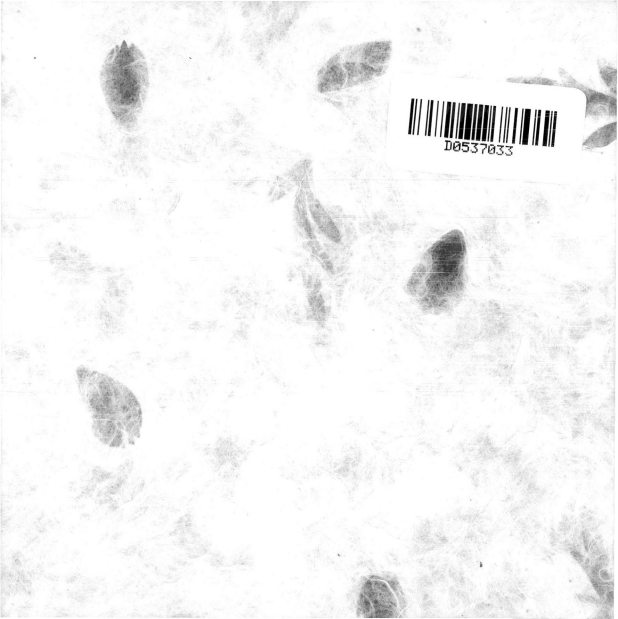

The "Language of" Series...

Thoughts to Share with a
WONDERFUL
SON

A Blue Mountain Arts® Collection
Edited by Douglas Pagels

Blue Mountain Press ®

SPS Studios, Inc., Boulder, Colorado

Library of Congress Catalog Card Number: 98-46833
ISBN: 0-88396-489-9

ACKNOWLEDGMENTS appear on page 48.

Certain trademarks are used under license.

Manufactured in Thailand
Fourth Printing: April 2000

This book is printed on recycled paper.

Library of Congress Cataloging-in-Publication Data

Thoughts to share with a wonderful son : a Blue
Mountain Arts collection / edited by Douglas Pagels.
        p.   cm. --   ("Language of..." series)
   ISBN 0-88396-489-9 (alk. paper)
      1. Sons--Literary collection. I. Pagels, Douglas. II. SPS
Studios (Firm) III. Series.
   PN6071.S57 T48 1999
   306.874--dc21

                                          98-46833
                                          CIP
                                          Rev.

SPS Studios, Inc.

P.O. Box 4549, Boulder, Colorado 80306

Contents

(Authors listed in order of first appearance)

A Little Message with a Lot of Love

Sometimes we need
reminders in our lives
of how much people care.
If you ever get that feeling,
I want you to remember this...

I love you, Son.
Beyond words that can even begin
to tell you how much,
I hold you and your happiness
within my heart each and every day.

I am so proud of you, and so thankful
to the years that have given me
so much to be thankful for.

If I were given a chance to be
anything I wanted to become,
there's nothing I would rather be
        ...than your parent.

And there is no one
I would rather have
        ...as my son.

        ☆ Douglas Pagels

Parents' hearts are always
with their children.

ᛉ Anonymous

There is a secret laughter
        That often comes to me,
And though I go about my work
        As humble as can be,
There is no prince...
            I envy — no, not one.
No evil can befall me —
        By God, I have a son!

ᛉ Christopher Morley

I feel so fortunate to have you for a son
I love your bright face
when we talk seriously about the world
I love your smile
when you laugh at the inconsistencies in the world
I love your eyes
when you are showing emotion
I love your mind
when you are discovering new ideas
and creating dreams to follow
Many people tell me that
they cannot talk to their children
that they cannot wait for them to leave home
I want you to know
that I enjoy you so much and
I look forward to any time we can spend together
Not only are you my adored son
but you are also my friend
I am so proud of you
my son and
I love you

Susan Polis Schutz

A wise son makes a glad father.

☆ Proverbs 10:1 (NKJV)

There is an enduring tenderness in
the love of a mother to a son that
transcends all other affections of
the heart.

☆ Washington Irving

The Universe Changes When a Son Is Born

Last night my child was born — a very strong boy.
If you ever become a father, I think the strangest
and strongest sensation of your life will be hearing
for the first time the thin cry of your own child.
For a moment you have the strange feeling of being
double; but there is something more... perhaps the
echo in a man's heart of all the sensations felt by
all the fathers and mothers... at a similar instant
in the past....

No man can possibly know what life means, what
the world means, what anything means, until he
has a child and loves it. Then the whole universe
changes and nothing will ever again seem exactly
as it seemed before.

☆ Lafcadio Hearn

We never know the love of our parents
until we have become parents.

Henry Ward Beecher

To a Young Son

In your face I sometimes see
Shadowings of the man to be,
And eager, dream of what my son
Will be in twenty years and one.

But when you are to manhood grown,
And all your manhood ways are known,
Then shall I, wistful, try to trace
The child you once were in your face?

Julia Johnson Davis

Enjoy every moment while you are young.
Enjoy the flowers and the sunshine while
you can... get all out of every moment
that you can.

I want you to be happy every second.

Robert G. Ingersoll

The Way to Happiness

Keep your heart free from hate, your mind
free from worry. Live simply; expect little,
give much. Fill your life with love. Scatter
sunshine. Think of others, and do as you
would be done by.

Anonymous

Young men, you are the architects of your own fortunes. Rely upon your own strength of body and soul. Take for your star, self-reliance.... Keep at your helm and steer your own ship. Remember that the great art of commanding is to take a fair share of the work.

Think well of yourself.

☆ Porter

I Cannot Teach You

I cannot teach you, though the years
  Have led me farther on
Along the path of life than you
  In your short span have gone.

I can but lead you to the threshold
  Of your thinking mind,
And leave you there to search the worth
  Of such as you may find.

I can but point the way, then you
  Must travel your road alone;
The crossroads you will meet will not be
  Those that I have known...

The rest is up to you,
  The choice is yours to make —
And I can only pray that 'tis
  The right road you will take.

                              Helen Lowrie Marshall

If I had influence with the good fairy
who is supposed to preside over the
christening of all children, I should ask
that her gift to each child in the world
be a sense of wonder so indestructible
that it would last throughout life.

Rachel Carson

The great man is he who does
not lose his child's heart.

Mencius

Every child walks into existence
through the golden gate of love.

— Henry Ward Beecher

Purpose

I do not know what we are here for upon
this wonderful and beautiful earth, this
incalculably interesting earth, unless it is
to crowd into a few short years every
possible fine experience and adventure;
unless it is to live our lives to the uttermost;
unless it is to seize upon every fresh
impression, develop every latent capacity;
unless it is to grow as much as ever we
have it in our power to grow.

— David Grayson

Work hard, be as good a scholar as you are a good boy, and love your father, who is always thinking about you.

☆ Victor Hugo

Nobody knows what a boy is worth,
and the world must wait and see;
for every man in an honored place
is a boy that used to be.

☆ Anonymous

To keep the body in good health is a
duty... otherwise we shall not be able
to keep our mind strong and clear.

⭐ Buddha

When I think of the sorrows and regrets
of my life, not one of them is associated
with the times I've stopped working and
took time off to play.

⭐ Robert Fulghum

A Son Is...

...the shining light of his parents' hopes and dreams. He is a young man who makes life's moments so beautiful with the miracle of all that he has been, and the treasure of everything he will become.

Terry Bairnson

...someone who will never be too grown up
for me to put my arms around.

Millie P. Lorenz

...a baby who is wished wondrous love; a child who is wished endless joy; a boy who is wished understanding and ever-widening circles of knowledge and friendship.

...a teenager who is wished strength in any surroundings, courage in every circumstance, and a recognition of the wonders that await his tomorrows.

...and a man, with paths to walk, with bridges to cross, with mountains to climb. A son is an amazing combination of all of these things, and he's quietly thanked, every day of his life, for the priceless joy he brings.

Douglas Pagels

...your past and your future...
your hopes and your dreams.

Barbara Cage

...the inspiration for so many joyful images
blending together through the years: of growing
so wonderfully, in body and mind; of learning
the real meaning of love; of the closeness that
truly defines a family.

Lorrie Westfall

...a gift that makes its presence known, to the
thankful heart of a parent, each and every day.

Anna Tafoya

...a boy that bears a striking resemblance
to a dream come true.

L. N. Mallory

Every survival kit includes
a sense of humor.

☆ Anonymous

Before I got married I had six theories
about bringing up children. Now I have
six children and no theories.

☆ John Wilmot

The best thing about living at home is
the way your parents worry about you.
Of course, they have *reason* to worry
about you. They know you.

☆ Bill Cosby

No man believes genius is hereditary
until he has a son.

✩ Anonymous

Ever-Changing Perspectives

The vantage points from which a son views his life and his parents view him are never fixed positions. They're always in motion, especially during a son's teenage years.

A little patience goes a long way, and, as Samuel Butler said, "The one serious conviction a man should have is that nothing should be taken too seriously." One saying reminds us that "A boy becomes an adult three years before his parents think he does — and about two years after he thinks he does!" And, as a reminder of how things change, one need look no further than the words of Mark Twain: "When I was a boy of fourteen, my father was so ignorant I could hardly stand to have the old man around. But when I got to be twenty-one, I was astonished at how much the old man had learned in those seven years."

Recipe for Growing Boys

Take one boy, about seven pounds. Give to a family who loves him very much. Simmer together with laughter, patience, comfort and a deep sense of responsibility for about three years. Let season, but watch carefully for signs of spoiling.

Mix one part firmness with two parts understanding. Add both at the same time, with mature wisdom. Let season. Then mix thoroughly the Golden Rule with some baseball, fishing trips, responsibilities, privacy, picnics, games and a cookie jar. Shake in some soap, toothpaste and a comb.

Now very slowly add some good books, some music, a football, a lawn mower and a savings account. Let season quite awhile. Then mix liberally with some dreams that make sense and some that don't; some for fun and some for growth. Stir in some good conversation about grades, honor, beliefs, love, patriotism, girls, cars and the World Series. Sprinkle with humor.... For extra interest, add a few roots such as integrity, fidelity, determination and gentleness. Mix with an interest in school activities, civic duty and his fellow man. Pour in some weekend jobs and a goal or two. Let season.

When you think he's ready, garnish with faith in tomorrow... and gaze with pride.

Irene Noble

I have nothing more at heart, my dear son, than your success and welfare, and the cultivation of your talents and virtues.

Daniel Webster

My dear boy... I am writing... with great love and a comfortable hope that your behavior will be such as to do yourself, and me, and your mother credit.... Take but a little trouble with yourself, and everyone will be delighted with you, and try to gratify you in all your reasonable wishes. And, above all, you will be at peace with yourself, and a double blessing to me... your fond father.

Samuel Taylor Coleridge

Son, This Is How It Works

Each day is a blank page in the diary of your life. The pen is in your hand, but the lines will not all be written the way you choose; some will come from the world and the circumstances that surround you. But for the many things that are in your control, there is something special you need to know.

Follow your dreams. Work hard. Be kind. This is all anyone could ever ask: Do what you can to make the door open on a day that is filled with beauty in some special way.

Remember: Goodness will be rewarded. Smiles will pay you back. Have fun. Find strength. Be truthful. Have faith. Don't focus on anything you lack.

Realize that people are the treasures in life, and happiness is the real wealth. Have a diary that describes how you are doing your best, and...

The rest will take care of itself.

☆ Douglas Pagels

Of Work Done Well

Never you mind the crowd, lad...
  Look where the millions stop;
You'll find the crowd at the base, lad;
  There's always room at the top.

Courage and faith and patience!
  There's space in the old world yet;
The better the chance you'll find, lad,
  The farther along you get.

Keep your eye on the goal, lad,
  Never despair or drop;
Be sure that your path points upward —
  There's always room at the top.

☆ George Thomas Dowling

There is in this world
no such force
as the force of a man
determined to rise.

W. E. B. DuBois

The potential of a child is the most
intriguing thing in all creation.

Ray Lyman Wilbur

Growing Up

The urge of growth is the creative urge,
the creative power in the universe. It lights
enthusiasm... and the fire within us is fed
by the life around us and we get into the
current of that life.

Richard C. Cabot

If my father's child can get to be president, your father's child can make his heart's desire.

Abraham Lincoln

After long experience in sizing up people, I definitely know you have the goods and you can go a long way. Now, aren't you foolish not to get all there is out of what God has given you.... I would be lacking — if I did not urge you to take advantage of the qualities you have.... I am always urging you to do the best you can.

Joseph P. Kennedy,
writing to his son, John F. Kennedy

Selections from "Letters to My Son"
by Lord Chesterfield

As Grenville Kleiser notes, "It was Lord Chesterfield's fondest desire that his son should be a real gentleman.... To this end he wrote his famous 'Letters.' These intimate personal letters, not originally intended for publication, can be read by young men today with great benefit, since they talk of principles... as enduring as the stars." These excerpts are taken from those 18th-century letters:

All that is worth the trouble of doing at all deserves to be done well.

Encourage ambition and continue to deserve the praises of the praiseworthy.

Let my experience supply you and clear your way in the progress of your youth of those thorns... which scratched me in the course of mine.

Deserve a great deal, and you shall
have a great deal.

Acquaint me sometimes with your studies,
sometimes with your diversions; tell me of any
new persons and characters that you meet with,
and add your own observations upon them.

Do not be discouraged by the first difficulties.

Never be ashamed nor afraid of asking questions.

Study the mind and heart of man,
and begin with your own.

There is nothing which I more wish that you
should know, and which fewer people do know,
than the true use and value of time....
I recommend to you to take care of the
minutes; for hours will take care of themselves.

☆ ☆

If I can't always be there in person, then...
I'll just have to put in letters what we would
have talked about were we together.... I'm no
Lord Chesterfield, but I'll try...

Think of all that has occurred in your
lifetime, let alone that of your dad.
And think of all that will come in the
years ahead... developments in medicine,
science, communication, computers,
transportation, etc., etc., etc. And you
will be there to see it and — more than
that — you will be prepared to benefit
from each of the developments to come.
How lucky you are. What a wonderful
time to be alive and young.

John Broome

Of one thing be sure, young gentlemen: this and the next few years hold great possibilities.... Changed and changing conditions will develop. Things will have to be done in a new way, and the man with the new idea will have the best chance....

What men *want* to do, they *can* do.

— Arthur Brisbane

My dear son... you have arrived at years capable of improving under the advantages you will be likely to have, if you do but properly attend to them.... Great learning and superior abilities, should you possess them, will be of little value and small estimation, unless virtue, honor, truth and integrity are added to them.

☆ Abigail Adams

Oh, youth, go forth and do!
You too, to fame may rise;
You can be strong and wise.
Stand up to life and play the man,
You can if you'll just think you can;
The great were once as you.

You envy them their proud success?
'Twas won with gifts that you possess.

☆ Edgar A. Guest

Big shots are little shots
who kept shooting.

☆ Christopher Morley

Have patience with everything that remains unsolved in your heart. Try to love the questions themselves.... Do not now look for the answers. They cannot now be given to you because you could not live them. It is a question of experiencing everything. At present, you need to *live* the question. Perhaps you will gradually, without even noticing it, find yourself experiencing the answer, some distant day.

Rainer Maria Rilke

I Have a Boy to Bring Up

I have a boy to bring up. Help me to perform my task with wisdom, kindness, and good cheer. Help me always to see him clearly, as he is...

I have a boy to bring up. Give me great patience and a long memory. Let me remember the hard places of my own youth, so that I may help when I see him struggling as I struggled then. Let me remember the things that made me glad... lest I forget that a child's laughter is the light of life.

I have a boy to bring up. Teach me that love understands all things, knows no weakness, tolerates no selfishness.

I have a son to bring up... with the values of goodness and just rewards... and happiness.

Angelo Patri

Don'ts and Do's

Don't ever stop dreaming your dreams;
   they're a very essential part of you.
Do whatever you can to make them
   a reality — by the course you take,
      the plans you make,
         and all the things you do.
Don't try to accomplish everything at
   once; life can be difficult enough
   without adding frustration to the list.
Do travel one step at a time, and reach
   for one goal at a time. That's the way
   to find out what real accomplishment is.
Don't be afraid to do the impossible, even
   if others don't think you'll succeed.
Do remember that history is filled with
   the incredible accomplishments of those
      who were foolish enough... to believe.

☆ Collin McCarty

Can'ts and Cans

If you would have some worthwhile plans
You've got to watch your can'ts and cans;
You can't aim low and then rise high;
You can't succeed if you don't try;
You can't go wrong and come out right;
You can't love sin and walk in light;
You can't throw time and means away
And live sublime from day to day.

☆ Anonymous

Do the thing that is right
even when the boss isn't looking,
because the boss isn't a criterion.

The real boss is standing alongside you
every moment of your life.

Alfred P. Haake

Don't try for perfection. Trying
to be good enough will be plenty.

Mitzi McClosky

My challenge to the young people is to pick up where this generation has left off, to create a world where every man, woman and child is not limited, except by their own capabilities.

Colin Powell

The whole secret of life is to be interested in one thing profoundly, and in a thousand things well.

Hugh Walpole

A Father's Wishes for His Son

Son, may you find happiness in every direction your paths take you. May you never lose that sense of wonder you have always had, and may you hold on to the sense of humor you use to brighten the lives of everyone who knows you. May you go beyond the ordinary steps and discover extraordinary results. May you keep on trying to reach for your stars, and may you never forget how wonderful you are. May you be rewarded with the type of friendships that get better and better — and the kind of love that blesses your life forever. May you go out of your way to stay healthy in body and soul, and may you know what it takes to deal with the stress of living in what is sometimes a difficult world. May you never lose your ability to see your way through to the other side of any worries. May you share your beautiful spirit with others, and remember how much magic a smile can provide.

Son, may you meet every challenge you are faced with, recognize every precious opportunity, and be blessed with the knowledge that you have the ability to make every day special. May you search for serenity, and discover it was within you all along. May you be strong enough to keep your hopes and dreams alive. May you always be gentle enough to understand. May you know that you hold tomorrow within your hands, and that the way there will be shared with the makings of what will be your most wonderful memories. And may you always remember, each step of the way…

You are loved, Son, more than words can ever begin to say.

☆ R. L. Keith

A Mother Sees Her Son

Sometimes when I watched you climb a tree,
I didn't see the determination in your eyes —
only your clumsiness and tattered shorts
   from the fall you shortly took.
I was thinking ruined shorts.
You were thinking mountains.

Sometimes when you rode your bike and
   jumped your ramp in frolicsome danger,
I didn't see the bravery in your deed —
only the impending, foolhardy scar.
I was thinking emergency room.
You were thinking power and speed.

Sometimes when a grade was slipping
   and I feared failure, I didn't see
the other grades that were super —
only the bad one.
I was thinking it was my failure.
You were just thinking.

Some twenty years have come and gone,
and you have grown to be a young man.
I can see the power of your dreams,
   the height of your optimism, and
   the speed of your accomplishments.
Sometimes I just didn't see.

But I can now.

☆ Pat W. Pugh-Stanley

To My Son

When you were very, very small
I used to dance with you cradled in my arms
You were my precious angel
And holding you close
Love overwhelmed me

I wondered what kind of a life you would lead
What would be your first word, your first job
What kind of a man you would become
And if your life would take you far from me

And I'd hold you even closer
Giving you an extra kiss, an extra hug
And whispering "I love you" one more time
Knowing you were too small to remember
But, praying you would never forget

There are days when I long to hold you
In my arms and dance once again

Although I miss my little boy
I am so proud of everything you are
And of the man you will become
My love for you still overwhelms me

As we both grow older
Please never forget
What you were too small... to remember.

Kathryn Higginbottom Gorin

I hope my son looks back upon today
And sees a mother who had time to play.
Whether the work was done, or it was not;
Who realized chores are sometimes best forgot.
There will be years for
    cleaning house and cooking,
But little boys grow up when we're not looking.

Barbara Overton Christie

We are so very glad that you are happy...
long may you keep so, my dear boy....
May you go on as well
as you have begun.

Charles Darwin

To My Son, with Love

A mother tries to provide her son
with insight into the important things in life
in order to make his life
as happy and fulfilling as possible

A mother tries to teach her son
to be kind and generous towards other people
to be honest and forthright at all times
to be fair, treating men and women equally
to respect and learn from older people
to know himself very well
to understand his strong and weak points
to accept criticism and learn from his mistakes
to have many interests to pursue
to have many goals to follow
to work hard to reach these goals

A mother tries to teach her son
to have a strong set of beliefs
to listen to his intelligence
to laugh and enjoy life
to appreciate the beauty of nature
to express his feelings openly
   and honestly at all times
to realize that love is the best emotion
   that anyone can have
to value the family unit
   as the basis of all stability

If I have provided you with an insight
into most of these things
then I have succeeded as a mother
in what I hoped to accomplish in raising you
If many of these things slipped by
while we were all so busy
I have a feeling that you know them anyway
And as a proud mother and as a friend
I will always continue to love and support
everything you are and everything you do
I am always here for you, Son
I love you

☆ Susan Polis Schutz

ACKNOWLEDGMENTS

We gratefully acknowledge the permission granted by the following authors, publishers, and authors' representatives to reprint poems or excerpts from their publications.

Philosophical Library for "Enjoy every moment..." by Robert G. Ingersoll. Copyright © 1951 by Eva Ingersoll Wakefield. All rights reserved. Reprinted by permission of Philosophical Library, New York.

Thomas Nelson Publishers for "Young men,..." by Porter from BETTER THAN GOLD by Clinton T. Howell. Copyright © 1970 by Clinton T. Howell. All rights reserved. Reprinted by permission.

HarperCollins Publishers, Inc. for "When I think..." from WORDS I WISH I WROTE by Robert Fulghum. Copyright © 1997 by Robert Fulghum. All rights reserved. Reprinted by permission.

Doubleday, a division of Random House, Inc., for "The best thing..." from FATHERHOOD by Bill Cosby. Copyright © 1986 by William H. Cosby, Jr. All rights reserved. Reprinted by permission.

Marilyn Moore & Associates, Inc. for "After long experience..." by Joseph P. Kennedy. Copyright © 1968 by The C. R. Gibson Co. All rights reserved. Reprinted by permission.

Warner Books, Inc. for "If I can't..." by John Broome from LETTERS FROM DAD by John C. Broome with John C. (Jack) Broome, II. Copyright © 1996 by John Broome and John C. (Jack) Broome, II. All rights reserved. Reprinted by permission.

New World Library for "Have patience..." from LETTERS TO A YOUNG POET by Rainer Maria Rilke. Copyright © 1998 by New World Library. All rights reserved. Reprinted by permission of New World Library, Novato, CA.

Sue Bender for "Don't try for..." by Mitzi McClosky from EVERYDAY SACRED by Sue Bender, published by HarperSanFrancisco, a division of HarperCollins Publishers. Copyright © 1995 by Sue Bender. All rights reserved. Reprinted by permission.

Pat W. Pugh-Stanley for "A Mother Sees Her Son." Copyright © 1999 by Pat W. Pugh-Stanley. All rights reserved. Reprinted by permission.

Kathryn Higginbottom Gorin for "To My Son." Copyright © 1999 by Kathryn Higginbottom Gorin. All rights reserved. Reprinted by permission.

The Trustees of the Wedgwood Museum for "We are so very..." by Charles Darwin from EMMA DARWIN, A CENTURY OF LETTERS 1792-1896 edited by Henrietta Litchfield, published by D. Appleton-Century Company, Inc., New York. Copyright © by Henrietta Litchfield. All rights reserved. Reprinted by permission.

A careful effort has been made to trace the ownership of poems and excerpts used in this anthology in order to obtain permission to reprint copyrighted materials and give proper credit to the copyright owners. If any error or omission has occurred, it is completely inadvertent, and we would like to make corrections in future editions provided that written notification is made to the publisher:

SPS STUDIOS, INC., P.O. Box 4549, Boulder, Colorado 80306.